Zero to Ninety Nine

Problem Solving on a 100 Square

Zero to Ninety Nine

Problem Solving on a 100 Square

By Noel Graham and Janine Blinko

Illustrated by Sascha Lipscomb

Claire Publications

©Noel Graham and Janine Blinko

First Published 1989
Second Impression 1990
Third Impression 1993
Published by
Claire Publications
Unit 8
Tey Brook Craft Centre
Great Tey
Colchester
Essex CO6 1JE
England.
ISBN 1-871098 02 5

Printed in Great Britain by
Hollen Street Press Ltd,
Slough, Berkshire

TABLE OF CONTENTS

Page

Foreword --------------------------------- vii

Introducing the Number Square ----------- 1

0 to 99 Games --------------------------- 19

Guess my Rule --------------------------- 43

Calculations and Patterns ----------------- 55

FOREWORD

The numbers we use most frequently are those between 0 and 100.
Our money and measurement systems are all designed to change
whenever 100 is reached e.g. 100 centimetres in a metre. It is vital
we give children an ease and familiarity with this set of numbers.

The patterns that exist in these numbers are best seen when
they are laid out in a 10 by 10 square which we call a 100 square.
The activities in this book use a square which begins at zero and
ends at ninety-nine. We appreciate that most commercially
available 100 squares use the numbers 1 to 100 and have therefore
placed one at the back of the book for teachers who prefer these
squares. All of the activities will work equally well on both
squares.

Our decision to use the 0 to 99 square has its foundations in the
belief that as children develop an understanding of our
sophisticated number system, the most important number they
encounter is zero. In addition to this the square which begins
with zero leads to a very convenient arrangement of numbers i.e.
all the single digit numbers are on the first line, all the tens
on the second line and so on.

0	1	2	3	4	5	6	7	8	9
10	11	12	13	14	15	16	17	18	19
20	21	22	23	24	25	26	27	28	29
30	31	32	33	34	35	36	37	38	39
40	41	42	43	44	45	46	47	48	49
50	51	52	53	54	55	56	57	58	59
60	61	62	63	64	65	66	67	68	69
70	71	72	73	74	75	76	77	78	79
80	81	82	83	84	85	86	87	88	89
90	91	92	93	94	95	96	97	98	99

INTRODUCING THE NUMBER SQUARE

ABOUT YOU

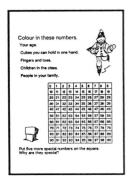

- -

This activity familiarises the children with the hundred square.

- -

Each child needs a copy of the sheet opposite and some crayons.

Ask the children to follow the instructions.

Some suggestions for special numbers might be:

- their house number
- their shoe size
- the number of cubes they can hold in one hand
- the number of people in their class with a pet dinosaur
- the number of people in their class who had toast for breakfast

Shade these numbers:

Your age.

Cubes you can hold in one hand.

Fingers and toes.

Children in the class.

People in your family.

0	1	2	3	4	5	6	7	8	9
10	11	12	13	14	15	16	17	18	19
20	21	22	23	24	25	26	27	28	29
30	31	32	33	34	35	36	37	38	39
40	41	42	43	44	45	46	47	48	49
50	51	52	53	54	55	56	57	58	59
60	61	62	63	64	65	66	67	68	69
70	71	72	73	74	75	76	77	78	79
80	81	82	83	84	85	86	87	88	89
90	91	92	93	94	95	96	97	98	99

Put five more special numbers on the square.
Why are they special?

PICTURES

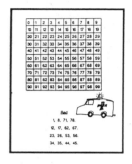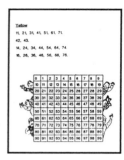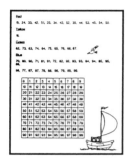

- -

This activity reinforces knowledge of the hundred square and encourages the children to look for patterns within it.

- -

Each child needs one or more of the following worksheets and some crayons.

<u>Using the worksheets with numbers</u>

Ask the children to find and mark the listed numbers.
Each set of numbers gives a picture on the 100 square.
Ask them to guess what the picture will be before they finish.

<u>Using the worksheets without numbers:</u>

Children can:
- design their own pictures to fit in with the given theme.
- write a set of instructions for their picture which they
  give to a friend to try.
  Will the two pictures look the same?

<u>Extension</u>

Each child designs a skyscraper to be used as a New York skyline collage.

0	1	2	3	4	5	6	7	8	9
10	11	12	13	14	15	16	17	18	19
20	21	22	23	24	25	26	27	28	29
30	31	32	33	34	35	36	37	38	39
40	41	42	43	44	45	46	47	48	49
50	51	52	53	54	55	56	57	58	59
60	61	62	63	64	65	66	67	68	69
70	71	72	73	74	75	76	77	78	79
80	81	82	83	84	85	86	87	88	89
90	91	92	93	94	95	96	97	98	99

Red

1, 8, 71, 78.

12, 17, 62, 67.

23, 26, 53, 56.

34, 35, 44, 45.

5

<u>Yellow</u>

11, 21, 31, 41, 51, 61, 71.

42, 43.

14, 24, 34, 44, 54, 64, 74.

16, 26, 36, 46, 56, 66, 76.

0	1	2	3	4	5	6	7	8	9
10	11	12	13	14	15	16	17	18	19
20	21	22	23	24	25	26	27	28	29
30	31	32	33	34	35	36	37	38	39
40	41	42	43	44	45	46	47	48	49
50	51	52	53	54	55	56	57	58	59
60	61	62	63	64	65	66	67	68	69
70	71	72	73	74	75	76	77	78	79
80	81	82	83	84	85	86	87	88	89
90	91	92	93	94	95	96	97	98	99

Red

15, 24, 33, 42, 51, 25, 34, 43, 52, 35, 44, 53, 45, 54, 55.

Yellow

16.

Green

62, 73, 63, 74, 64, 75, 65, 76, 66, 67.

Blue

70, 80, 90, 71, 81, 91, 72, 82, 92, 83, 93, 84, 94, 85, 95, 86, 96, 77, 87, 97, 78, 88, 98, 79, 89, 99.

0	1	2	3	4	5	6	7	8	9
10	11	12	13	14	15	16	17	18	19
20	21	22	23	24	25	26	27	28	29
30	31	32	33	34	35	36	37	38	39
40	41	42	43	44	45	46	47	48	49
50	51	52	53	54	55	56	57	58	59
60	61	62	63	64	65	66	67	68	69
70	71	72	73	74	75	76	77	78	79
80	81	82	83	84	85	86	87	88	89
90	91	92	93	94	95	96	97	98	99

0	1	2	3	4	5	6	7	8	9
10	11	12	13	14	15	16	17	18	19
20	21	22	23	24	25	26	27	28	29
30	31	32	33	34	35	36	37	38	39
40	41	42	43	44	45	46	47	48	49
50	51	52	53	54	55	56	57	58	59
60	61	62	63	64	65	66	67	68	69
70	71	72	73	74	75	76	77	78	79
80	81	82	83	84	85	86	87	88	89
90	91	92	93	94	95	96	97	98	99

0	1	2	3	4	5	6	7	8	9
10	11	12	13	14	15	16	17	18	19
20	21	22	23	24	25	26	27	28	29
30	31	32	33	34	35	36	37	38	39
40	41	42	43	44	45	46	47	48	49
50	51	52	53	54	55	56	57	58	59
60	61	62	63	64	65	66	67	68	69
70	71	72	73	74	75	76	77	78	79
80	81	82	83	84	85	86	87	88	89
90	91	92	93	94	95	96	97	98	99

MAKE IT
A game for 2 players

- -

This game develops calculating skills.

- -

You need the worksheet overleaf and some counters.

To play:

Players should:-

- choose a target number, for example 24.

- take it in turns to choose a number from the TOP LINE ONLY,
  place a counter on it and keep a record of it.
  It may not be chosen again by either player.

- add the next chosen number to the original and keep a running total.
  The first player to reach the target number wins the game.

Ask questions like:-

> Can you make up a rule for overshooting the target?
> What is the easiest way to keep track of your score?
> Is there a way to win?
> Is it best to start first or second?
> Can you keep a joint total instead of separate totals?
  The winner is the player to reach the target during their turn.

Variations and Extensions

1. Players choose four numbers each from the square, two of which must be greater than the target.
They use them to make the target number.
Numbers may be used more than once.
Any operation may be used.
The winner is the player who gets closest to the target after 6 turns.

2. Discuss with the children how the game could be changed.
They may suggest:
- the first player over the target wins.
- change the target.
- any numbers less than the target may be chosen.
- subtraction may be used of players are forced beyond the target.
- using a die to select numbers.

Children should be asked to:
- decide between them how they will change their rules.
- play the new game to see if it works.

It is essential that the children devise and try their own rules, and make their own decisions about whether or not theirs is a good game.

The children write down instructions for their game, and give them to some friends to follow. If their instructions are not clear enough, children can negotiate with the authors for more precise instructions.

MAKE IT

0	1	2	3	4	5	6	7	8	9
10	11	12	13	14	15	16	17	18	19
20	21	22	23	24	25	26	27	28	29
30	31	32	33	34	35	36	37	38	39
40	41	42	43	44	45	46	47	48	49
50	51	52	53	54	55	56	57	58	59
60	61	62	63	64	65	66	67	68	69
70	71	72	73	74	75	76	77	78	79
80	81	82	83	84	85	86	87	88	89
90	91	92	93	94	95	96	97	98	99

FIND THE NUMBERS
a game for two players

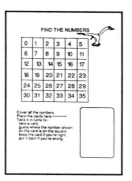

- -

This activity encourages the understanding of place value and pattern

- -

Each pair of children need a copy of the worksheet overleaf, a set of 0-99 cards and some counters.

<u>To play</u>

Cover all the numbers on the square with counters.
Shuffle the cards and place them face down on the worksheet.

Players take it in turns to:

- take a card from the top of the pile

- work out where that number is without looking under the counters

- remove the counter which covers the number they think is the right one

- if they are correct they keep the card, if not, it is replaced.

After ten turns each the player with the most cards wins the game.

<u>Variations and Extensions</u>

1. Use a 6 x 6 grid (see worksheet on page 15) and a set of 0-35 cards.

2. Play the game on other grids (see the back of the book).

FIND THE NUMBERS

Cover all the numbers.
Place the cards here $\longrightarrow$
Take it in turns to:-
  take a card,
    guess where the number shown
    on the card is on the square,
    keep the card if you're right,
    put it back if you're wrong.

0	1	2	3	4	5	6	7	8	9
10	11	12	13	14	15	16	17	18	19
20	21	22	23	24	25	26	27	28	29
30	31	32	33	34	35	36	37	38	39
40	41	42	43	44	45	46	47	48	49
50	51	52	53	54	55	56	57	58	59
60	61	62	63	64	65	66	67	68	69
70	71	72	73	74	75	76	77	78	79
80	81	82	83	84	85	86	87	88	89
90	91	92	93	94	95	96	97	98	99

FIND THE NUMBERS

0	1	2	3	4	5
6	7	8	9	10	11
12	13	14	15	16	17
18	19	20	21	22	23
24	25	26	27	28	29
30	31	32	33	34	35

Cover all the numbers.
Place the cards here ———————➤
Take it in turns to:-
 take a card,
 guess where the number shown
 on the card is on the square,
 keep the card if you're right,
 put it back if you're wrong.

FIND THE MULTIPLES
A game for 2-4 players

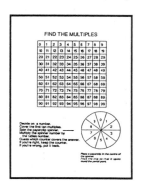

- -

This activity encourages children to learn, recall and use multiplication facts.

- -

Groups need one copy of the 'Multiples' worksheet opposite, a paperclip and some counters.

Ask the children to play the game described on the worksheet.

Variations and Extensions

1. Play the same game with all multiples of the chosen number covered.

2. Play the same game with every number covered.

3. Change the game:
   Cover all the numbers. Players take it in turns to:
      - spin a number.
      - guess where there is a number hidden that the spinner number will divide into without a remainder.
      - if they are right, they keep the counter.
      - the first player with 10 counters wins the game.

4. Ask the children to invent a new game.

5. See 'Multiple Patterns'.

16

FIND THE MULTIPLES

0	1	2	3	4	5	6	7	8	9
10	11	12	13	14	15	16	17	18	19
20	21	22	23	24	25	26	27	28	29
30	31	32	33	34	35	36	37	38	39
40	41	42	43	44	45	46	47	48	49
50	51	52	53	54	55	56	57	58	59
60	61	62	63	64	65	66	67	68	69
70	71	72	73	74	75	76	77	78	79
80	81	82	83	84	85	86	87	88	89
90	91	92	93	94	95	96	97	98	99

Decide on a number.
Cover the first ten multiples.
Spin the paperclip spinner. ➡
Multiply the spinner number by
  the tables number.
Guess which counter covers the answer.
If you're right, keep the counter.
If you're wrong, put it back.

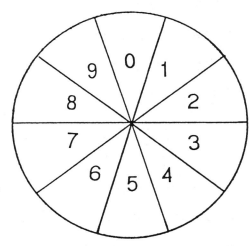

Place a paperclip in the centre of the spinner.
Flick the clip so that it spins round the pencil point.

0	1	2	3	4	5	6	7	8	9
10	11	12	13	14	15	16	17	18	19
20	21	22	23	24	25	26	27	28	29
30	31	32	33	34	35	36	37	38	39
40	41	42	43	44	45	46	47	48	49
50	51	52	53	54	55	56	57	58	59
60	61	62	63	64	65	66	67	68	69
70	71	72	73	74	75	76	77	78	79
80	81	82	83	84	85	86	87	88	89
90	91	92	93	94	95	96	97	98	99

0-99 GAMES

4 IN A ROW
A game for two or more players

- -
This activity encourages skills in mental arithmetic and place value.
- -

You need a copy of the worksheet opposite, two dice or two paperclip spinners (see page 77) and counters for each player.

To play:

- players take it in turn to throw the dice
- the two numbers thrown are used are used to make as many numbers as possible
  e.g. if the dice are rolled to give,

| 2 | 5 |

the following scores are possible:

25   using the 2 in the tens place, and 5 in the units place,
52   using the 5 in the tens place and 2 in the units place,
10   2 x 5
7   2 + 5
3   5 - 2
5
2

> The numbers made are covered with counters

> The first player with a line of 4 adjacent counters in any direction, wins the game.

20

FOUR IN A ROW

0	1	2	3	4	5	6	7	8	9
10	11	12	13	14	15	16	17	18	19
20	21	22	23	24	25	26	27	28	29
30	31	32	33	34	35	36	37	38	39
40	41	42	43	44	45	46	47	48	49
50	51	52	53	54	55	56	57	58	59
60	61	62	63	64	65	66	67	68	69
70	71	72	73	74	75	76	77	78	79
80	81	82	83	84	85	86	87	88	89
90	91	92	93	94	95	96	97	98	99

You need two dice or spinners.
Take it in turns.
Throw the dice.
Make as many numbers as you can.
Cover them with counters.
The first player with 4 counters in a row wins.

BINGO
A game for a group or a class

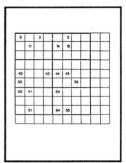 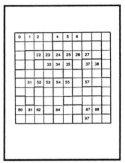

- -
This activity familiarises children with the square, encourages them to look for patterns, and develops their understanding of place value.
- -

You need:- a large blank 100 square to record the numbers called, and
a set of Bingo cards.
(Each card is a section of a 100 square and can be made by cutting along the thick black lines on the worksheets. Two class sets are available.

To play:-

- One child is chosen as caller and another to record the numbers called on the blank 100 square.
- Each player has a bingo card with three 'give-away' numbers.
- The caller shuffles the set of 0-99 cards, and then begins by taking the top card and calling it out to the rest of the group.
- Players write this number on their card if it belongs there.
- Play continues as the Caller reads out each card in turn.
- The winner is the first player to complete their card. (or a row to make a quicker game)

Variations and Extensions

1. The caller uses the paperclip spinner (see back of book).
Two numbers are spun. Players use them to make as many of the numbers on their card as they can.
For example, 9 and 4 will make 36 (4 x 9), 13 (4 + 9), etc.

0		2			5				
	11			14	15				
40			43	44	45				
50						56			
60	61			64					
	81			84	85				

	11	12	13						
					25	26	27		
	31	32	33						
						46	47	48	
					75	76	77		
	81	82	83						

		2		4			7	
				14		16	17	
		42				46	47	
				54	55	56		
			63	64		66		
					75	76	77	

20	21			24						
		32		34	35					
			43	44	45					
		62	63	64						
			73		75	76				
			83	84						
			93							

		22	23	24		26			
						36		38	
		42	43			46			
				55			57	58	
				75	76	77			
					96	97	98		

0	1	2		4	5	6			
		22	23	24	25	26	27		
			33	34	35		37	38	
	51	52	53	54	55		57		
80	81	82		84			87	88	
							97		

28

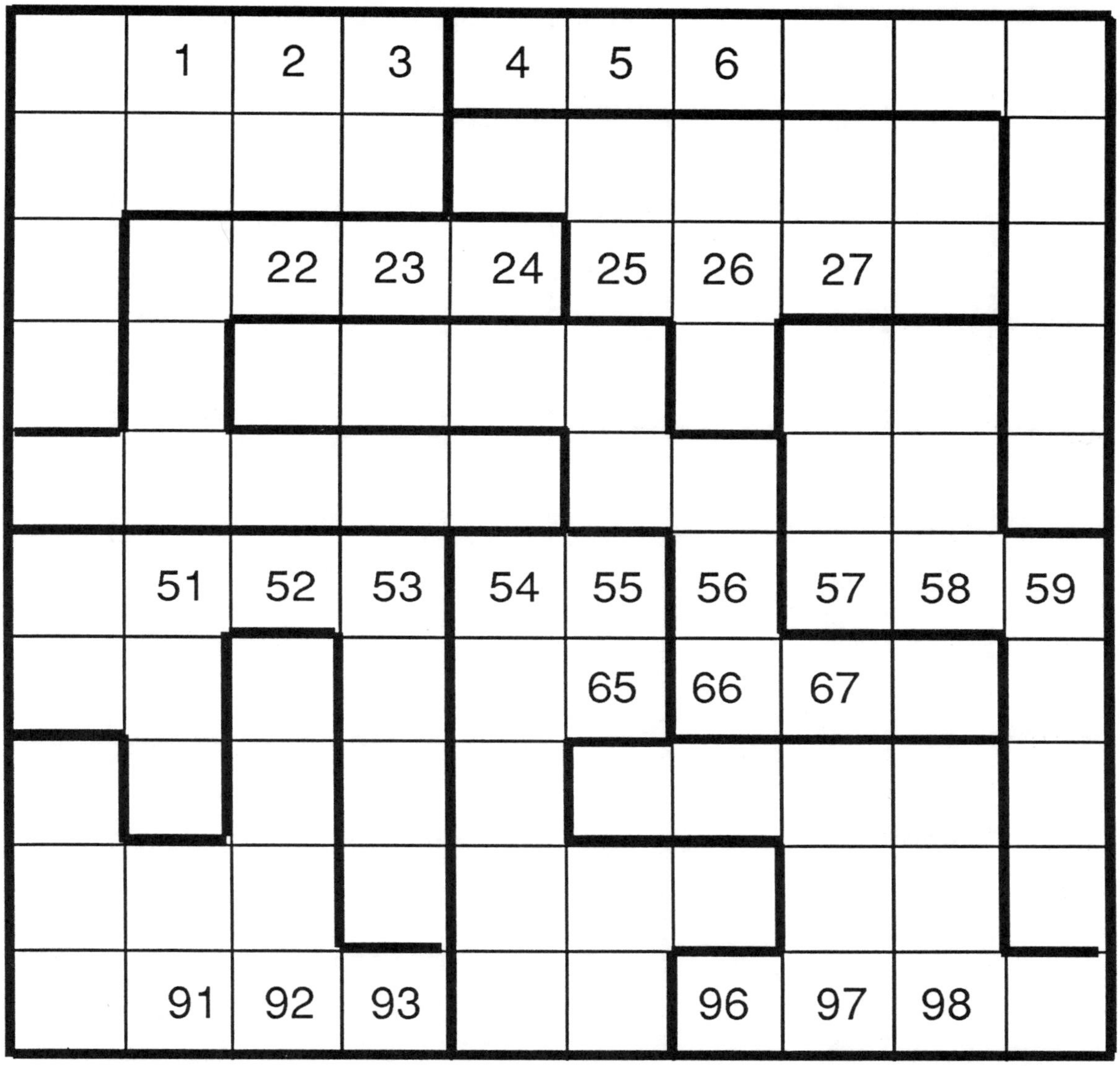
1 2 3 4 5 6
22 23 24 25 26 27
51 52 53 54 55 56 57 58 59
65 66 67
91 92 93 96 97 98

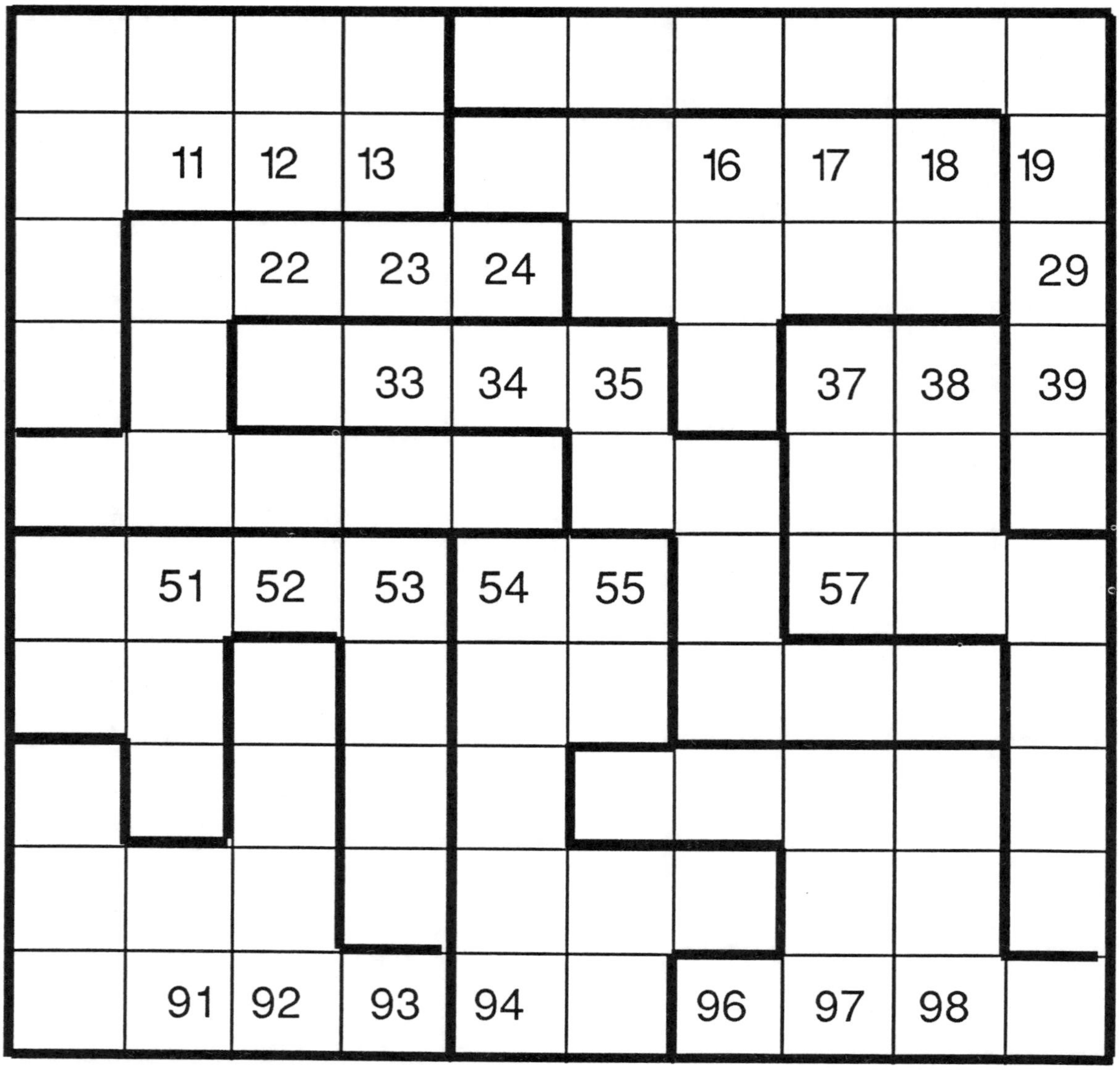
11 12 13 16 17 18 19
22 23 24 29
33 34 35 37 38 39
51 52 53 54 55 57
91 92 93 94 96 97 98

MOVING ABOUT

- -

This activity encourages children to look for pattern

- -

You need: 100 squares
worksheets overleaf

<u>To play</u>:

Ask the children what they think 21↑ means.

Accept whatever answers they offer.

Then ask them what 21 ↑ ↑ means.

Agree on a standard interpretation, which will probably be that ↑ means to move up one square ie. from 21 to 11.

Follow the same process for other possibilities ↓ → ← ↗ ↙ ↘ ↖

Use the worksheets overleaf.

<u>Variations and Extensions</u>

1. Specify how many arrows may be used to get from one number to another.

2. Given a set of arrows eg

Which numbers is it possible to use as a starting place on the 100 square. For example, it is possible to begin at 27 and end at 85; it is not possible to begin at 62, because the arrows send you off the board!

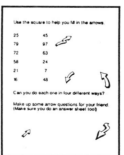

Use a hundred square to solve these problems.

1. 21 → →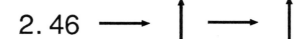

2. 46 → ↑ → ↑

3. 44 → ↑ ← ↓

4. 53 ↓ ↓ ↓

5. 98 ← ← ↑

6. 80 → → ↑ ↑

7. 56 ← ↓ ← ↓

8. 6 ↓ ↓ ← ←

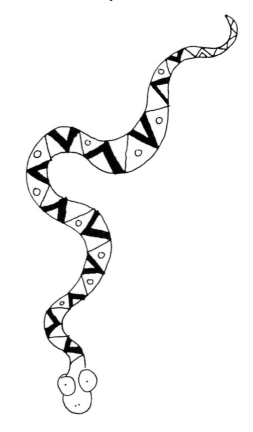

Explain as a sum what each arrow does.

_____

_____

_____

_____

Use a hundred square to solve these problems.

1. 2

2. 73

3. 65 /

4. 62

5. 33 ↘ ↗ ↘

6. 87 ↘ ↗ ↑

7. 25 ↘ ↘

8. 95 ↑ ↑ ↑

Explain as a sum what each arrow does.

_____

_____

_____

_____

Use the square to help you fill in the arrows.

25	45
79	97
72	63
58	24
21	7
16	48

Can you do each one in four different ways?

Make up some arrow questions for your friend.
(Make sure you do an answer sheet too!)

A MOVING ABOUT INVESTIGATION

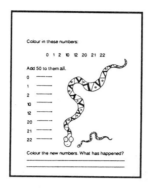

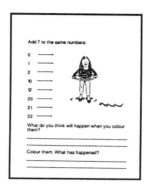

- -

This activity is an extension of 'Moving About'.

- -

The children need hundred squares and the following two worksheets.

Ask the children to follow the directions on the worksheets, find out what is happening to the shape they draw.

<u>Variations and Extensions</u>

1. Specify where the original square must go.
   Ask the children to write the instructions.
   For example,

> " Find a way to make the square touch 99.
>   Explain how you do it."

2. Suggest a shape for children to create on the hundred square.
   Specify where it must start and move to.
   Ask them to write the instructions.
3. Ask children to send their shape to 3 different places on the 100 square.
   For example,

> " Draw a 2 x 2 square that touches number 3 .
>   What numbers have you chosen?
>
> Make your square move to 52, then 83, then 25.
>   How did you do it?"

Shade these numbers:

0 1 2 10 12 20 21 22

Add 50 to them all.

0 ——————→

1 ——————→

2 ——————→

10 ——————→

12 ——————→

20 ——————→

21 ——————→

22 ——————→

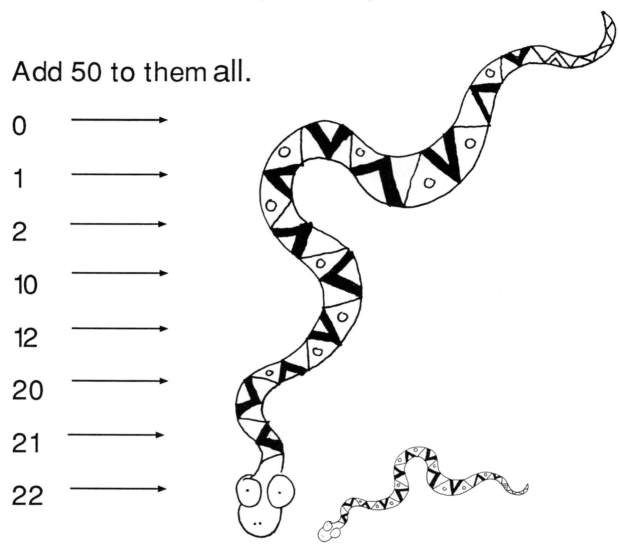

Shade the new numbers. What has happened?

_____

_____

Add 7 to the same numbers:

0   ——————▶

1   ——————▶

2   ——————▶

10   ——————▶

12   ——————▶

20   ——————▶

21   ——————▶

22   ——————▶

What do you think will happen when you shade them?

_____

_____

What happened when you did?

_____

_____

GUESS MY NUMBER

- -

This activity develops an understanding of place value and pattern.

- -

To play:

- One child/leader chooses a number on the hundred square and secretly writes
  it on a piece of paper.

- The rest of the class/group must discover what that number is by asking the
  leader questions.
  The leader may only answer 'Yes' or 'No'.

- The child who guesses the correct number becomes leader for the next round.

Ask questions like:-
       - Which questions are most useful?
       - Which questions get you closest to the answer?

Making the game simpler

> Play the above/below game.
  Use a record chart, record their
  guesses in the appropriate column.

Above	Below

> After each question, discuss which numbers can be eliminated, cross them
  out or cover them with a counter.
  Which questions eliminate more than one number?

> Only use part of the square, eg. 0 to 49.

Variations and Extensions

1. Limit the number of questions that may be asked.

2. Stipulate a minimum amount of numbers to be eliminated with each question. Discuss which questions eliminate most? least? one half or one quarter of the numbers?

3. Play as a team game. Award points for the number of numbers eliminated and 10 bonus points for guessing the correct number.

4. Stipulate words that must be used. For example, 'more', 'between', 'odd', 'multiple'.
   Award extra points for using them. For example, 5 points for using 'multiple', 10 points for 'divisible'.

5. Ask the children to devise a strategy to find the secret number as quickly as possible, ie. What is the best set of questions?

6. Find groups of questions which eliminate the same set of numbers.

7. How many questions are there which eliminate every number?

39

GUESS MY NUMBER

0	1	2	3	4	5	6	7	8	9
10	11	12	13	14	15	16	17	18	19
20	21	22	23	24	25	26	27	28	29
30	31	32	33	34	35	36	37	38	39
40	41	42	43	44	45	46	47	48	49
50	51	52	53	54	55	56	57	58	59
60	61	62	63	64	65	66	67	68	69
70	71	72	73	74	75	76	77	78	79
80	81	82	83	84	85	86	87	88	89
90	91	92	93	94	95	96	97	98	99

MULTIPLES
A game for two players

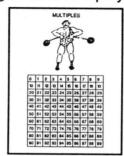

- -
This activity gives children an opportunity to learn and practise multiplication facts.
- -

You need: a die or paperclip spinner (see page 77), a hundred square between two players and different snaded counters for each player.

It may be useful if children have played 'Find the Multiples' as an introduction to this game.

To play:

>Players take it in turns to -throw the die
                              -place a counter on a multiple of the number thrown
>Children may use a calculator to help them calculate if they wish.
  The constant function on some calculators may be useful.
>The winner is the first player to get four of their counters in a horizontal,
  vertical or diagonal line.

Ask questions like:-

- How can you win?
  Discuss possible strategies, let children try them out.
- Can you block each other?
- Which numbers are easier to work out?
- Can you change the rules?
  Children may choose to use two dice to give larger multiples,
      or cover two multiples at each turn,
      or use a hundred square each,
      or make the winning shape a square, or any other shape.

MULTIPLES

0	1	2	3	4	5	6	7	8	9
10	11	12	13	14	15	16	17	18	19
20	21	22	23	24	25	26	27	28	29
30	31	32	33	34	35	36	37	38	39
40	41	42	43	44	45	46	47	48	49
50	51	52	53	54	55	56	57	58	59
60	61	62	63	64	65	66	67	68	69
70	71	72	73	74	75	76	77	78	79
80	81	82	83	84	85	86	87	88	89
90	91	92	93	94	95	96	97	98	99

0	1	2	3	4	5	6	7	8	9
10	11	12	13	14	15	16	17	18	19
20	21	22	23	24	25	26	27	28	29
30	31	32	33	34	35	36	37	38	39
40	41	42	43	44	45	46	47	48	49
50	51	52	53	54	55	56	57	58	59
60	61	62	63	64	65	66	67	68	69
70	71	72	73	74	75	76	77	78	79
80	81	82	83	84	85	86	87	88	89
90	91	92	93	94	95	96	97	98	99

GUESS MY RULE

GUESS MY RULE 1
A game for a group of children or a whole class.

| All the numbers which end in three. |
| Multiples of three. |
| Numbers more than 55, and less that 66. |
| Numbers whose digits add to 7. |
| Numbers which end in 3 or 4. |
| Multiples of 11. |
| Numbers where both digits are the same. |

| All the numbers in the 20's. |
| Even numbers. |
| Numbers less than 11. |
| Numbers whose digits add to over 10. |
| Numbers with a 4 in them. |
| Multiples of 5. |
| Numbers with only 2's or 3's in them. |

| All the numbers which end in 5. |
| Odd numbers. |
| Numbers more than 79. |
| Numbers whose digits add to 7. |
| Numbers with a 6 in them. |
| Multiples of 10. |
| Numbers between 37 and 45. |

This activity encourages children to look for patterns, and to manipulate number

The children need hundred squares (or one large one for a group to use) and rule cards made from the worksheets overleaf.

To play:

- The leader chooses a rule card, for example, 'All the numbers which end with 5', which the other children may not see.
- The leader shades all the numbers which fit that rule.
- The other children try to guess what the rule is.
- The child who guesses correctly becomes leader for the next round.

Suggestions and questions

> Which rules use the most numbers?
> Which rules use more than 10 numbers?
> Which rules use the fewest numbers?
> Which rules are easiest to guess? Why?
> Make some new rule cards.
> Invent a rule which fills the last two rows.
> Find some rules which use all the cards.
> Find rules which use no numbers/half the numbers.
> Find three different rules which generate the same set of numbers.
> Play in reverse. Begin with a blank 100 square and fill it in with numbers.

Extension

Each child chooses a rule, shades in the numbers which fit the rule and writes it on the back of their own square,
Squares are pinned on the classroom wall.
Children try to identify the rule for each square.

GUESS MY RULE

0	1	2	3	4	5	6	7	8	9
10	11	12	13	14	15	16	17	18	19
20	21	22	23	24	25	26	27	28	29
30	31	32	33	34	35	36	37	38	39
40	41	42	43	44	45	46	47	48	49
50	51	52	53	54	55	56	57	58	59
60	61	62	63	64	65	66	67	68	69
70	71	72	73	74	75	76	77	78	79
80	81	82	83	84	85	86	87	88	89
90	91	92	93	94	95	96	97	98	99

All the numbers which end in three.

Multiples of three.

Numbers more than 55, and less than 66.

Numbers whose digits add to 7.

Numbers which end in 3 or 4.

Multiples of 11.

Numbers where both digits are the same.

All the numbers in the 20's.

_____

Even numbers.

_____

Numbers less than 11.

_____

Numbers whose digits add up to over 10.

_____

Numbers with a 4 in them.

_____

Multiples of 5.

_____

Numbers with only 2's or 3's in them.

All the numbers which end in 5.

_____

Odd numbers.

_____

Numbers more than 79.

_____

Numbers whose digits add up to 7.

_____

Numbers with a 6 in them.

_____

Multiples of 10.

_____

Numbers between 37 and 45.

GUESS MY RULE 2
A game for a group of children or a whole class.

more	less
same	between
multiple	end
begin	digits

- -

This activity assumes that children have played the game in 'GUESS MY RULE 1'. It encourages them to look for patterns, and to invent rules.

- -

To play:

- The aim of this game is to invent rules.
- Children take it in turns to give a rule, eg. 'There is a 2 in the number'.
- Numbers to which this rule applies are marked with a pen or a counter.
- The game ends when all the numbers have been marked,

Variations

1. Limit the number of rules, eg. 'All the numbers must be marked in no more than 10 rules.'

2. Specify the number of rules eg. 'Use exactly 8 rules to mark all the numbers.'

3. Specify the types of rules that can be used, eg. 'They must all be "more than" rules.

4, Cut the worksheet on page 51 into separate cards.
Shuffle them and turn them face-down.
Children take the top card and invent a rule which includes that word (or words).
Extend the game by asking them to take 2 cards and use them both in their rule.

Extensions

1. Use one of the number squares at the back of the book.
   Ask children to invent and record rules which account for all the numbers.

2. How many different rules can children invent which account for 10 numbers?
   Can they invent a rule which accounts for 4 numbers?
   Try other sets of numbers.

5. Give points according to the words that are used in the rules.
   For example: 'multiple' gives 10 points, 'more' gives 5 points.
   Who can score the most with 5 rules?

more	less
same	between
multiple	end
begin	digits

WHO AM I?

Language or mathematics?

You will need a 100 square.
                Counters
                The worksheet overleaf.

- -

This activity encourages children to use mathematical language and to reason logically.

- -

The answers to the riddles can all be found on the 0-99 square.
Ask the children to:
- Use the square to eliminate impossible answers.
  For example,

My tens digit is one more
than my units digit.
I am odd.
I am divisible by 5.
Who am I?

The first statement tells us that,

My tens digit is one more than my units digit.

Numbers can be eliminated from the 0-99 square which do not fall into this category, by either crossing them out or covering them with a counter.

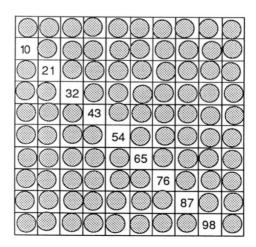

And similarly with the second statement,

I am odd.

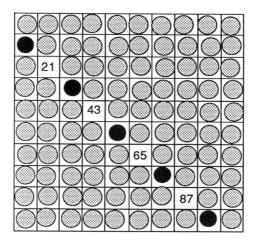

And the third,

I am divisible by 5

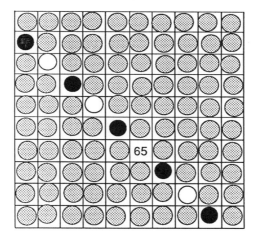

When the answer becomes apparent.

<u>Variations and Extensions</u>

>Ask questions which demand a range of answers.
>Use a smaller grid and lower answers.
>Ask children to make up their own riddles for their friends to solve.

One of my digits is odd
One is even
Their product is less than 24,
but greater than 18
What two numbers might I be?

I am the largest two-digit number whose units digit divides the tens digit evenly!

My tens digit is one more than my units digit.
I am odd.
I am divisible by 5.
Who am I?

The sum of my digits is the same as the product of my digits.
Who am I?

My digit product is 10.
I am even.
Who am I?

My digits are the same.
Their sum is 3 less then their product.
Who am I?

The sum of my digits is ten.
Their difference is two.
I am less than fifty.
Who am I?

The sum of my digits is 2.
I am greater than 12.
Who am I?

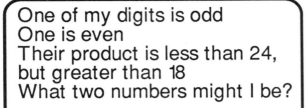

0	1	2	3	4	5	6	7	8	9
10	11	12	13	14	15	16	17	18	19
20	21	22	23	24	25	26	27	28	29
30	31	32	33	34	35	36	37	38	39
40	41	42	43	44	45	46	47	48	49
50	51	52	53	54	55	56	57	58	59
60	61	62	63	64	65	66	67	68	69
70	71	72	73	74	75	76	77	78	79
80	81	82	83	84	85	86	87	88	89
90	91	92	93	94	95	96	97	98	99

CALCULATIONS AND PATTERNS

THIS AND THE NEXT
A number investigation

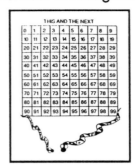

. . . .

This investigation encourages children to :
- **look for pattern,**
- **invent and test rules,**
- **calculate mentally,**
- **work systematically,**
- **collaborate.**

. . . .

Introducing the Activity

Teachers may choose to introduce this activity on a large hundred square and then let the children work in groups to investigate the problem on smaller squares.

Initial activity

Children take it in turns to:-
- choose a number
- add it to the next number
- find the answer on the square and cover it.
  (if the sum is not on the square. the child misses a turn)

After several numbers have been changed, ask some questions...
- Do you think there will be a pattern?
- What kind of pattern?
- Why do you think that?

*** Accept whatever answers the children offer.***

Continue until the pattern becomes apparent to the children (which may not be until it is complete) and ask...
"Why are only these numbers affected?"
"What's the rule?"

  It is essential that the children have plenty of time to reason this out

Making the investigation simpler
- Begin by only choosing numbers from the top two rows on the chart, then use subsequent rows one by one.
- Use a smaller grid eg. 6 x 6.

0	1	2	3	4	5
6	7	8	9	10	11
12	13	14	15	16	17
18	19	20	21	22	23
24	25	26	27	28	29
30	31	32	33	34	35

Extending the activity

1. a. Ask the children to explore what emerges when each number is added to the next two?

   Children will need plenty of time to investigate for themselves.
   A sequence of numbers will emerge.

   Ask questions like:-
   > Can you predict the tenth number in the sequence?
      .. the hundredth?...the millionth?
   > Can you describe the pattern in words?

   b. Add four consecutive numbers and record the results on the board.

   Ask children to make predictions as above

   c. Try other groups of numbers.
      Ask questions like:-
   > Can you predict what will happen with these groups of numbers.
   > Can you see a pattern with the first number in each set?

   d. Which numbers cannot be found by adding any number of consecutive numbers?

2. Investigate the patterns that emerge when different groups of numbers are added. For example, vertical or diagonal sets of numbers.

3. Ask the children to set tasks for each other. For example, 'Find three consecutive numbers which have a sum of 45'
   Is there a system for solving this type of problem?

THIS AND THE NEXT

0	1	2	3	4	5	6	7	8	9
10	11	12	13	14	15	16	17	18	19
20	21	22	23	24	25	26	27	28	29
30	31	32	33	34	35	36	37	38	39
40	41	42	43	44	45	46	47	48	49
50	51	52	53	54	55	56	57	58	59
60	61	62	63	64	65	66	67	68	69
70	71	72	73	74	75	76	77	78	79
80	81	82	83	84	85	86	87	88	89
90	91	92	93	94	95	96	97	98	99

PALINDROMIC NUMBERS
A number investigation

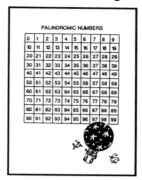

- -
This investigation gives children experience in looking for and using pattern, and an interesting way to practice addition.
- -

A palindromic number is one which reads the same from right to left, as it does from left to right.

For example,

53235, 818 and 222

> *How many are there on the 100 square?*
Let children decide for themselves about numbers on the top row.

Many numbers are a form of palindrome. For example, 23 is a one-step palindrome.

reverse it! ⟶
$$\begin{array}{r} 23+ \\ \underline{32} \\ 55 \end{array}$$
...a palindrome.

> *How many of these are on the 100 square?*

28 is a two-step palindrome:-

reverse it!
$$\begin{array}{r} 28+ \\ \underline{82} \\ 110+ \\ \underline{011} \\ 121 \end{array}$$
..one step

...two steps, a palindrome.

There are also three and four-step palindromes.

Ask the children to:

- identify which numbers are palindromes already.

- identify some one-step and two-step palindromes.

- predict where the rest might be.

- check the predictions.

- find and shade 3-step and 4-step palindromes.

- find any quick ways of finding the patterns.

Do all numbers eventually become palindromes in this way?

Why is there a pattern?

PALINDROMIC NUMBERS

0	1	2	3	4	5	6	7	8	9
10	11	12	13	14	15	16	17	18	19
20	21	22	23	24	25	26	27	28	29
30	31	32	33	34	35	36	37	38	39
40	41	42	43	44	45	46	47	48	49
50	51	52	53	54	55	56	57	58	59
60	61	62	63	64	65	66	67	68	69
70	71	72	73	74	75	76	77	78	79
80	81	82	83	84	85	86	87	88	89
90	91	92	93	94	95	96	97	98	99

MULTIPLE PATTERNS

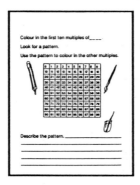
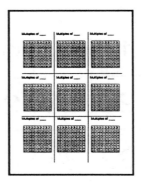

- -

This activity develops a knowledge of multiplication facts, and explores the relationships between them.

- -

Ask the children to generate and record patterns of multiples on the hundred square.
There are a number of ways to do this.

1. Use the worksheet opposite.
   They can 'collect' multiples on the second sheet.
   This can be done as a group or individually.

2. Use the constant function on a calculator.
   Ask the children if they can make the calculator count.
   Most calculators have a constant function.
   By pressing 1 + = = = = = the calculator will continue adding one to the previous number, ie. it will count.

   Use this function to make the calculator count backwards from 50.
   Make it count in twos, threes etc.

   Children can record the numbers generated when they are creating these multiples on a 100 square by placing a cube on each number displayed.
   For example, if the calculator is adding in sixes, the following numbers will be covered:- 0, 6, 12, 18, 24, 30, 36... etc
   The worksheet overleaf can be used to record this.

3. Use number rods or interlocking cubes to build the patterns.

Shade the first ten multiples of _____ .

Look for a pattern.

Use the pattern to shade the other multiples.

0	1	2	3	4	5	6	7	8	9
10	11	12	13	14	15	16	17	18	19
20	21	22	23	24	25	26	27	28	29
30	31	32	33	34	35	36	37	38	39
40	41	42	43	44	45	46	47	48	49
50	51	52	53	54	55	56	57	58	59
60	61	62	63	64	65	66	67	68	69
70	71	72	73	74	75	76	77	78	79
80	81	82	83	84	85	86	87	88	89
90	91	92	93	94	95	96	97	98	99

Describe the pattern. _____

_____

_____

_____

_____

Multiples of ___

0	1	2	3	4	5	6	7	8	9
10	11	12	13	14	15	16	17	18	19
20	21	22	23	24	25	26	27	28	29
30	31	32	33	34	35	36	37	38	39
40	41	42	43	44	45	46	47	48	49
50	51	52	53	54	55	56	57	58	59
60	61	62	63	64	65	66	67	68	69
70	71	72	73	74	75	76	77	78	79
80	81	82	83	84	85	86	87	88	89
90	91	92	93	94	95	96	97	98	99

Multiples of ___

0	1	2	3	4	5	6	7	8	9
10	11	12	13	14	15	16	17	18	19
20	21	22	23	24	25	26	27	28	29
30	31	32	33	34	35	36	37	38	39
40	41	42	43	44	45	46	47	48	49
50	51	52	53	54	55	56	57	58	59
60	61	62	63	64	65	66	67	68	69
70	71	72	73	74	75	76	77	78	79
80	81	82	83	84	85	86	87	88	89
90	91	92	93	94	95	96	97	98	99

Multiples of ___

0	1	2	3	4	5	6	7	8	9
10	11	12	13	14	15	16	17	18	19
20	21	22	23	24	25	26	27	28	29
30	31	32	33	34	35	36	37	38	39
40	41	42	43	44	45	46	47	48	49
50	51	52	53	54	55	56	57	58	59
60	61	62	63	64	65	66	67	68	69
70	71	72	73	74	75	76	77	78	79
80	81	82	83	84	85	86	87	88	89
90	91	92	93	94	95	96	97	98	99

Multiples of ___

0	1	2	3	4	5	6	7	8	9
10	11	12	13	14	15	16	17	18	19
20	21	22	23	24	25	26	27	28	29
30	31	32	33	34	35	36	37	38	39
40	41	42	43	44	45	46	47	48	49
50	51	52	53	54	55	56	57	58	59
60	61	62	63	64	65	66	67	68	69
70	71	72	73	74	75	76	77	78	79
80	81	82	83	84	85	86	87	88	89
90	91	92	93	94	95	96	97	98	99

Multiples of ___

0	1	2	3	4	5	6	7	8	9
10	11	12	13	14	15	16	17	18	19
20	21	22	23	24	25	26	27	28	29
30	31	32	33	34	35	36	37	38	39
40	41	42	43	44	45	46	47	48	49
50	51	52	53	54	55	56	57	58	59
60	61	62	63	64	65	66	67	68	69
70	71	72	73	74	75	76	77	78	79
80	81	82	83	84	85	86	87	88	89
90	91	92	93	94	95	96	97	98	99

Multiples of ___

0	1	2	3	4	5	6	7	8	9
10	11	12	13	14	15	16	17	18	19
20	21	22	23	24	25	26	27	28	29
30	31	32	33	34	35	36	37	38	39
40	41	42	43	44	45	46	47	48	49
50	51	52	53	54	55	56	57	58	59
60	61	62	63	64	65	66	67	68	69
70	71	72	73	74	75	76	77	78	79
80	81	82	83	84	85	86	87	88	89
90	91	92	93	94	95	96	97	98	99

Multiples of ___

0	1	2	3	4	5	6	7	8	9
10	11	12	13	14	15	16	17	18	19
20	21	22	23	24	25	26	27	28	29
30	31	32	33	34	35	36	37	38	39
40	41	42	43	44	45	46	47	48	49
50	51	52	53	54	55	56	57	58	59
60	61	62	63	64	65	66	67	68	69
70	71	72	73	74	75	76	77	78	79
80	81	82	83	84	85	86	87	88	89
90	91	92	93	94	95	96	97	98	99

Multiples of ___

0	1	2	3	4	5	6	7	8	9
10	11	12	13	14	15	16	17	18	19
20	21	22	23	24	25	26	27	28	29
30	31	32	33	34	35	36	37	38	39
40	41	42	43	44	45	46	47	48	49
50	51	52	53	54	55	56	57	58	59
60	61	62	63	64	65	66	67	68	69
70	71	72	73	74	75	76	77	78	79
80	81	82	83	84	85	86	87	88	89
90	91	92	93	94	95	96	97	98	99

Multiples of ___

0	1	2	3	4	5	6	7	8	9
10	11	12	13	14	15	16	17	18	19
20	21	22	23	24	25	26	27	28	29
30	31	32	33	34	35	36	37	38	39
40	41	42	43	44	45	46	47	48	49
50	51	52	53	54	55	56	57	58	59
60	61	62	63	64	65	66	67	68	69
70	71	72	73	74	75	76	77	78	79
80	81	82	83	84	85	86	87	88	89
90	91	92	93	94	95	96	97	98	99

THE SIEVE OF ERATOSTHENES

- -

This activity helps to develop an understanding of multiples, factors and prime numbers.

- -

Eratosthenes was a famous Greek mathematician. He invented the first known method of finding prime numbers. This activity is based on his work.

You need the worksheet overleaf, plenty of interlocking cubes and maybe calculators.
Children need to be able to generate multiples (see 'Multiples' worksheet on page 42).

Eratosthenes' sieve

Ask the children to:-
- Put a red cube on <u>all</u> the multiples of 2.

- Put a blue cube on <u>all</u> the multiples of 3.
  If there is a red cube on a number already, put the blue cube on top.

- Repeat this, identifying all multiples of numbers to ten.

Ask questions like:-

> There are 3 cubes on number 12, what can you tell me about 12?

> Which number(s) have the most cubes on them?
  Why?

> What can you tell me about the numbers with no cubes on them?
  How many are there?
  Are there as many between 100 and 199?

ERATOSTHENES' SIEVE

0	1	2	3	4	5	6	7	8	9
10	11	12	13	14	15	16	17	18	19
20	21	22	23	24	25	26	27	28	29
30	31	32	33	34	35	36	37	38	39
40	41	42	43	44	45	46	47	48	49
50	51	52	53	54	55	56	57	58	59
60	61	62	63	64	65	66	67	68	69
70	71	72	73	74	75	76	77	78	79
80	81	82	83	84	85	86	87	88	89
90	91	92	93	94	95	96	97	98	99

DIGITS

- -

This activity explores the digits that make up the numbers on the 100 square.

- -

Pupils need the worksheet overleaf.

Ask the children to:-

1. Estimate how many digits there are on the 100 square?
   Find at least two different ways of counting them.

2. Find out how many numbers contain only even digits? Odd digits?
   How many contain both odd and even digits?
   Express these results as percentages.

3. Find the sum of all the digits on the square.

4. Find the digital root of each number.
   For example, the digital root of 57 is 3. (5 + 7 = 12, 1 + 2 =3)
   Look for patterns.

5. Instead of adding the digits, multiply them.
   Look for patterns.

DIGITS

0	1	2	3	4	5	6	7	8	9
10	11	12	13	14	15	16	17	18	19
20	21	22	23	24	25	26	27	28	29
30	31	32	33	34	35	36	37	38	39
40	41	42	43	44	45	46	47	48	49
50	51	52	53	54	55	56	57	58	59
60	61	62	63	64	65	66	67	68	69
70	71	72	73	74	75	76	77	78	79
80	81	82	83	84	85	86	87	88	89
90	91	92	93	94	95	96	97	98	99

GAUSS
Following in the footsteps of a great mathematician

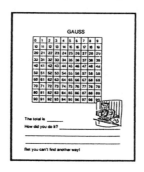

- -

This activity investigates ways different sets of numbers can be added.

- -

Pupils should have available any calculating device they might need, including 100 squares and calculators.

Introductory Activity.

Give the pupils a 100 square and ask them to add up all the numbers on it, THE QUICK WAY. Telling the story below can serve as a useful introduction.

'The story is told of a mathematics teacher fortunate (or unfortunate) enough to have a pupil named Gauss. Gauss was to become one of the most influential mathematicians this world has produced. The teacher asked his pupils to add together all the numbers from 0 to 100, hoping to keep them busy for a while. Gauss solved the problem in 2 minutes.'
How was it done?

For younger or less
numerate pupils limit
the activity to the first
few lines.

Pupils should be left to their own devices and encouraged to share their ideas with others. A range of different solutions will emerge , some of which are listed below:-

1.   i.   Add up all the numbers on the first row.
      ii. Add up the numbers on the second row, third row etc.
      iii. Add up the separate totals.
2. Do the same as in 1 but with the columns.
3. $1 + 99 = 100$, $2 + 98 = 100$, ...$48 + 52 = 100$, $49 + 51 = 100$. .....plus 50.
4. The 99th triangular number.

Many more methods exist. Much of the excitement that comes from doing this activity with pupils is the different methods they develop.

Extensions

Ask the children to use or adapt their methods to solve the following problems:-

1. Add up the even or odd numbers to 100.
2. Add up all the numbers to 1000, 10,000 or 1,000,000.
3. Devise techniques for adding up other sets of numbers such as the multiples of 3.
4. Are there any ways of counting how many multiples?

GAUSS

0	1	2	3	4	5	6	7	8	9
10	11	12	13	14	15	16	17	18	19
20	21	22	23	24	25	26	27	28	29
30	31	32	33	34	35	36	37	38	39
40	41	42	43	44	45	46	47	48	49
50	51	52	53	54	55	56	57	58	59
60	61	62	63	64	65	66	67	68	69
70	71	72	73	74	75	76	77	78	79
80	81	82	83	84	85	86	87	88	89
90	91	92	93	94	95	96	97	98	99

The total is _____

How did you do it? _____

_____

_____

Bet you can't find another way!

THREES AND SIXES

Each child needs plenty of hundred squares (blank and numbered)

The children will need to have experimented with the patterns that are given by colouring multiples, as in the 'MULTIPLES' worksheet.

Ask them to:

1. Record the multiples of three on a hundred square and save it.

2. Use two more numbered squares.
   Place one directly on top of the other.

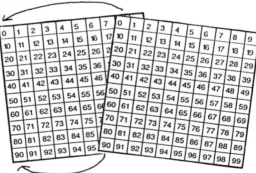

3. Find out which number lies directly beneath 0. (It is another 0!)
   Add those numbers together.
   Record the sum on the blank hundred square.

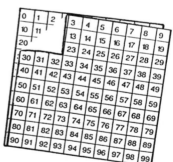

4. Do the same with each number on the square.
   Is there a pattern?

5. Record the multiples of three on this new square.
   What do you notice?
   Why does this happen?

72

Variations and Extensions

1. 'Add' three squares.
   Explore what happens to the multiples of three on the new chart.
   Try four or five squares.

2. Compare other multiple patterns on the new squares you have made.
   How do the multiples of two and four compare on the singles and doubles
   charts?

3. How many squares must be added to make the multiples of 7 produce a
   vertical pattern?

THE FINAL CHALLENGE

This rich activity develops the ability to see patterns and to think mathematically.

Children need plenty of hundred squares, blank and numbered.

Ask the children to:-

Place one square on top of another. (0 will be on top of 0)

1a. Turn the top square clockwise through 90⁰. (90 will now be on top of 0)
     Add the pairs of numbers on the first three lines. (90 + 0, 80 +1, etc)
     Record the results on a blank square.
     Complete the square using the number patterns on the first three lines.

b. Turn the top square through another 180⁰ (9 is now on top of 0).
    Add and record the pairs of numbers as in 1a.
    Compare the new square with the results from 1a.

2. This time, turn the top square so that 0 is on top of 99.
    Add and record the pairs of numbers as before.
    What do you notice?
    Can you use this result to find the sum of all the numbers from 0 to 99?
    (see 'Gauss' worksheet)

    Make this method work for other sets of numbers.
    For example, 0-10,000, all even numbers to 100.
    Invent a challenge.

0	1	2	3	4	5	6	7	8	9
10	11	12	13	14	15	16	17	18	19
20	21	22	23	24	25	26	27	28	29
30	31	32	33	34	35	36	37	38	39
40	41	42	43	44	45	46	47	48	49
50	51	52	53	54	55	56	57	58	59
60	61	62	63	64	65	66	67	68	69
70	71	72	73	74	75	76	77	78	79
80	81	82	83	84	85	86	87	88	89
90	91	92	93	94	95	96	97	98	99

To use the paperclip spinner :-

Place a paper and pencil in the centre of the spinner
Flick the clip so that it spins round the pencil point.

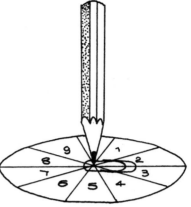

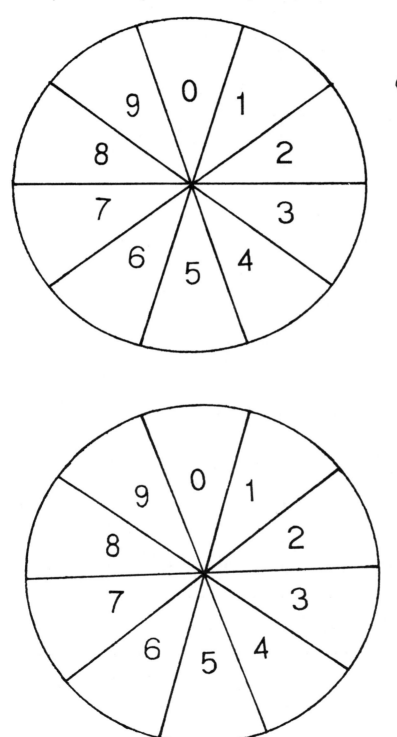

0	1	2	3
4	5	6	7
8	9	10	11
12	13	14	15

0	1	2	3	4	5	6	7	8
9	10	11	12	13	14	15	16	17
18	19	20	21	22	23	24	25	26
27	28	29	30	31	32	33	34	35
36	37	38	39	40	41	42	43	44
45	46	47	48	49	50	51	52	53
54	55	56	57	58	59	60	61	62
63	64	65	66	67	68	69	70	71
72	73	74	75	76	77	78	79	80

0	1	2	3	4
5	6	7	8	9
10	11	12	13	14
15	16	17	18	19
20	21	22	23	24

0	1	2	3	4	5	6	7
8	9	10	11	12	13	14	15
16	17	18	19	20	21	22	23
24	25	26	27	28	29	30	31
32	33	34	35	36	37	38	39
40	41	42	43	44	45	46	47
48	49	50	51	52	53	54	55
56	57	58	59	60	61	62	63

0	1	2	3	4	5
6	7	8	9	10	11
12	13	14	15	16	17
18	19	20	21	22	23
24	25	26	27	28	29
30	31	32	33	34	35

0	1	2	3	4	5	6
7	8	9	10	11	12	13
14	15	16	17	18	19	20
21	22	23	24	25	26	27
28	29	30	31	32	33	34
35	36	37	38	39	40	41
42	43	44	45	46	47	48

1	2	3	4	5	6	7	8	9	10
11	12	13	14	15	16	17	18	19	20
21	22	23	24	25	26	27	28	29	30
31	32	33	34	35	36	37	38	39	40
41	42	43	44	45	46	47	48	49	50
51	52	53	54	55	56	57	58	59	60
61	62	63	64	65	66	67	68	69	70
71	72	73	74	75	76	77	78	79	80
81	82	83	84	85	86	87	88	89	90
91	92	93	94	95	96	97	98	99	100

0	1	2	3	4	5	6	7	8	9
10	11	12	13	14	15	16	17	18	19
20	21	22	23	24	25	26	27	28	29
30	31	32	33	34	35	36	37	38	39
40	41	42	43	44	45	46	47	48	49
50	51	52	53	54	55	56	57	58	59
60	61	62	63	64	65	66	67	68	69
70	71	72	73	74	75	76	77	78	79
80	81	82	83	84	85	86	87	88	89
90	91	92	93	94	95	96	97	98	99

1	2	3	4	5	6	7	8	9	10
11	12	13	14	15	16	17	18	19	20
21	22	23	24	25	26	27	28	29	30
31	32	33	34	35	36	37	38	39	40
41	42	43	44	45	46	47	48	49	50
51	52	53	54	55	56	57	58	59	60
61	62	63	64	65	66	67	68	69	70
71	72	73	74	75	76	77	78	79	80
81	82	83	84	85	86	87	88	89	90
91	92	93	94	95	96	97	98	99	100

NOTES

NOTES

NOTES

NOTES